Eileen Kimbrough

Humanness

Micropoetry

ISBN: 978-0-692-67554-0

Cover design and art: Eileen Kimbrough
Inside art and poems: Eileen Kimbrough

Book design and editing: Eileen Kimbrough

Published by Half Moon Publications,
Aurora, Illinois

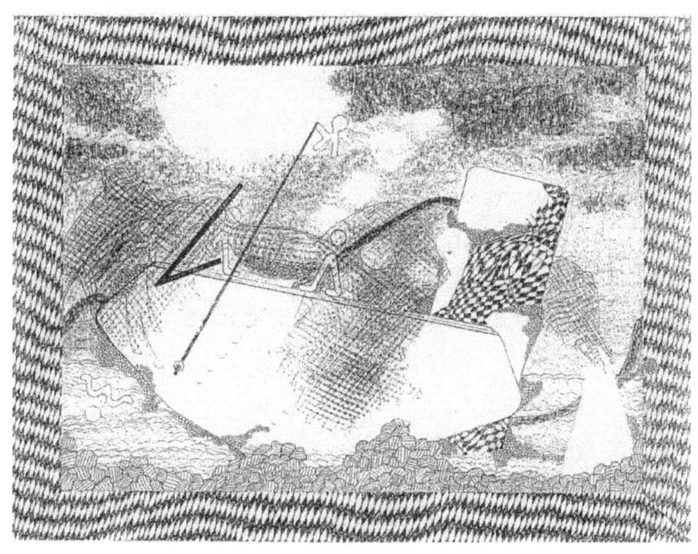

Humanness

In my studio, are faces,
    bodies, hands and feet
of people that I knew or know

They're on the walls
    and on the floor
Some are hidden in a file drawer

In these, I see ideas, gestures,
ways of humanness,
                the art of being,
      the being of art

Part One

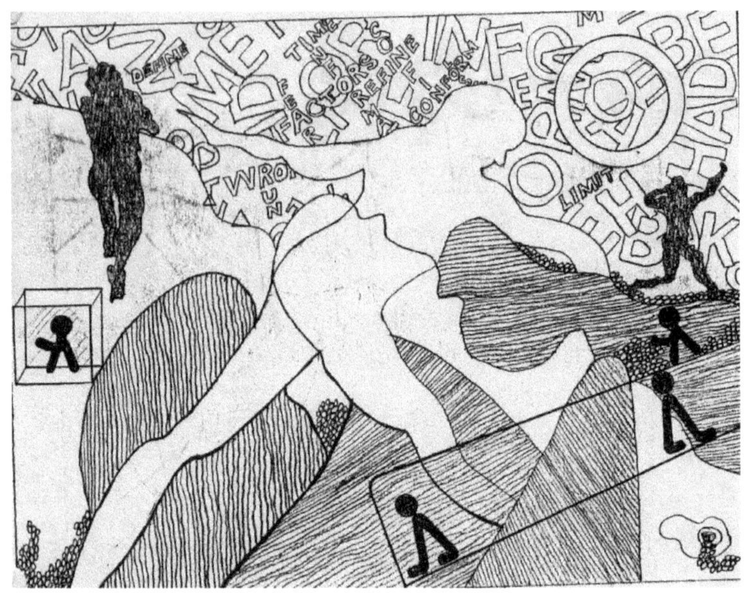
DEFINE
FACTORS
REFINE
CONFORM
LIMIT

The secret of the shadows?
Same as the fruit flies.
They come from nowhere
and return to never.
they exist for something else
but never really are.

* * *

Mud, rocks, puddles, dirt,
your child will find it,
little curious creature.

* * *

Stars…
  Small dots
  of soaring brilliance
  shine forever
  in my dreams.

Eileen Kimbrough

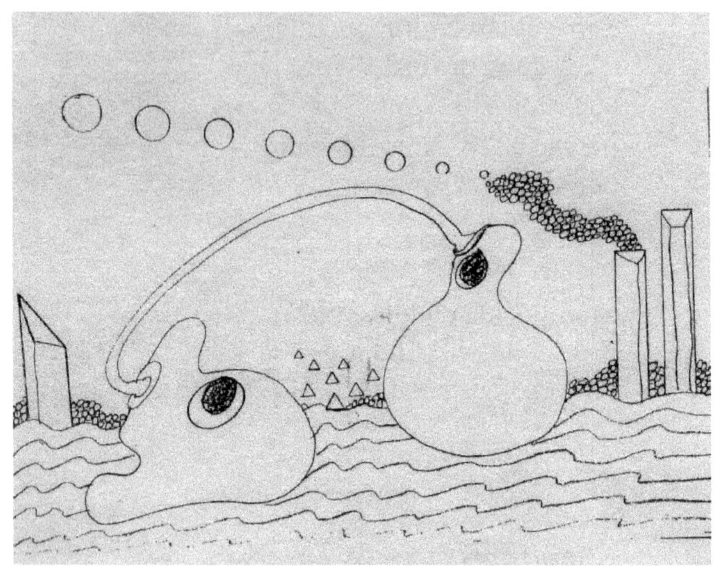

I turn over my shoe
    with the ant on top.
He walks around
    its sole.

* * *

Brother…

I see him once a year,
If that.

Who is that old man?
who used to build his dreams
in sand.

* * *

Reflections in the mirror.
Are they lying? I'd like to
wave a wand to change
my fragile reflection.

Eileen Kimbrough

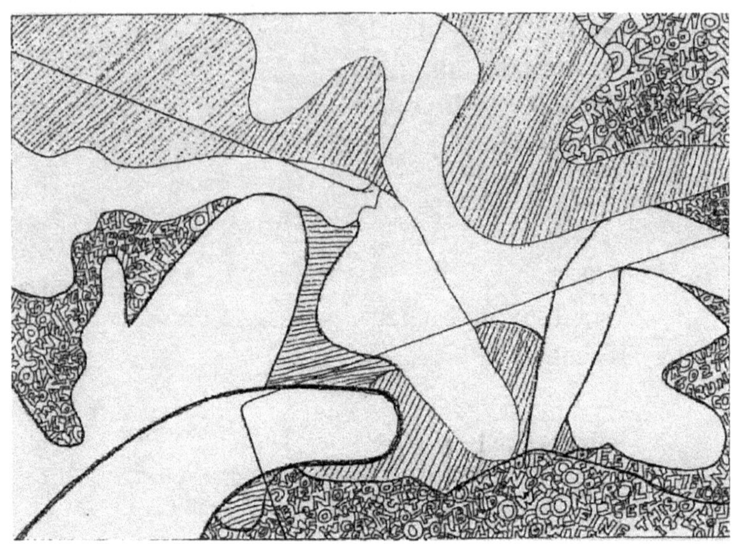

I am a connoisseur of words,
a lover of art and beauty,
would-be savior of nature, Earth, humanity.
And through all of these,
I am me.

* * *

Artists…
Place their dreams
on canvas,
bare their souls
for all to see,
portray the world
in special colors,
and search for ways
to help you find
your truth.

* * *

Pencil…
Sharp, smooth.
You preserve my touch.
Our marks
can then become words.
Or art.
To share. To keep.
To show the world
we care.

Eileen Kimbrough

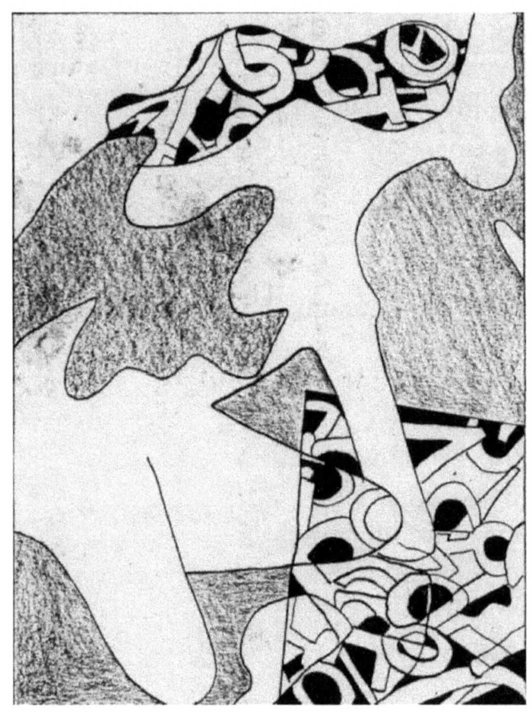

I want to rise like dawn
and see the whole universe
then sleep with the stars
and let the sun kiss my hands.
The moon will lead my way
and I will be one with all.

* * *

Broken moon…
shine your crooked light
on me this summer night.
Perfection doesn't mean
as much as being true.

* * *

My brain explodes,
a supernova,
like shattered glass
setting my spirit free.

Eyes of mannequins
    watching everyone-
        hidden cameras.

* * *

Keyhole,
curved top, tapered bottom,
you show me that I'm not welcome.
but I peek through,
a tiny view, mysterious, incomplete,
makes me wish for more…
or maybe less.

* * *

Windy day.
Strewn over streets and lawns,
    pieces of life.

Poetry…
a symphony of words
and emotion

* * *

Tortured souls with broken hearts
and saddened minds
write the best poems

* * *

Sometimes, late at night
when I'm in bed,
I write my best poems.
I always think I'll remember them.
And early mornings, poems form in my head
But when I find my writing tools
they are gone,
buried in some deep graveyard
in my mind.
They die while waiting.
They're killed by time.

Eileen Kimbrough

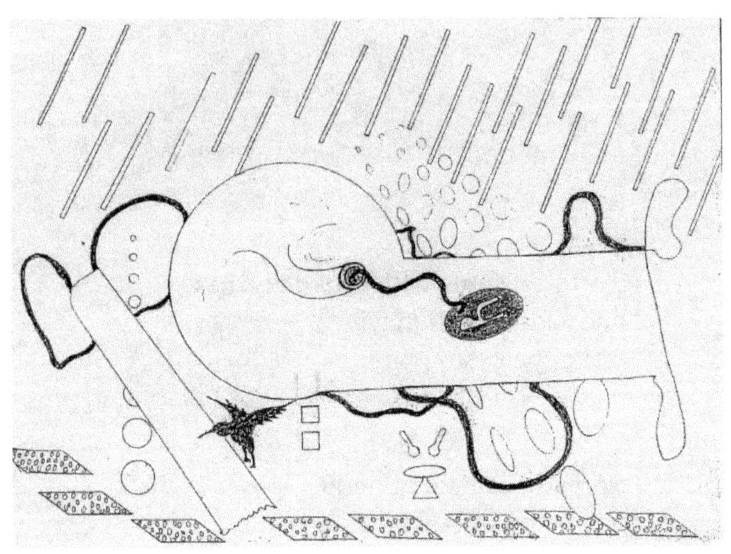

The cake on my fork,
seems small, tastes very good, yet,
            all those calories.

* * *

Yellow butter melting now
  on my bread with jelly, red
pretty little snack for me
  to eat before I go to bed

* * *

You know how the cookie tastes
                    when burned.
It's sweetness turns
                    to bitter.
Just like a lover, spurned.

Eileen Kimbrough

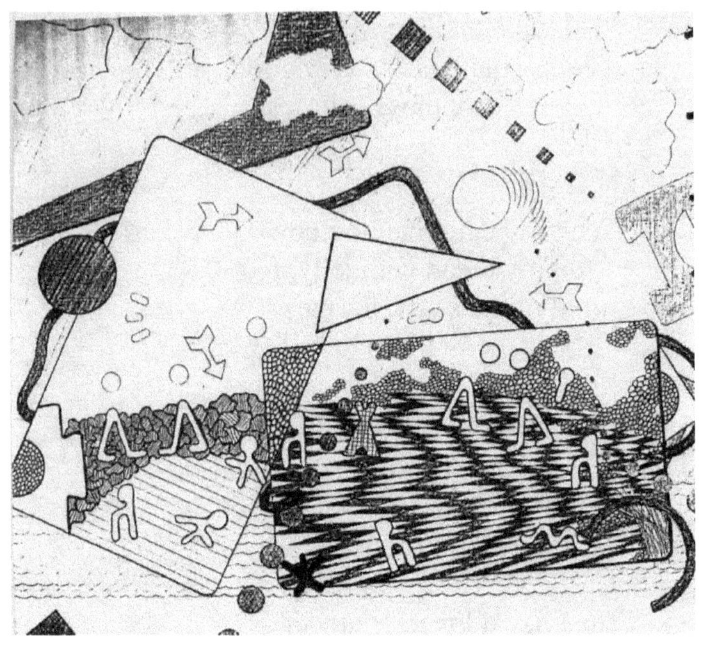

I read today's headlines
…toast is burning.

* * *

Duty
Plastic bag in hands,
behind his dog he stands.
What's happened to the human species,
that one has to carry his dog's feces?

* * *

Which Door
A slender woman passed me by,
and entered through Weight Watcher's door.
And I, as wide as I am high
walked into the ice-cream store next door.

Packing all the books
I planned to read
        but didn't.

* * *

Looking through the glass,
you seemed true
but when I put our drinks away,
I found the real you.

* * *

Oceans of water near
but I drown sorrow
in tears.

After the dentist,
  still numb,
  applying lipstick
      ...OOPS.

* * *

New décor...
  furniture
  painted with dust.

* * *

End of March
this rainy day
I do my taxes.

Eileen Kimbrough

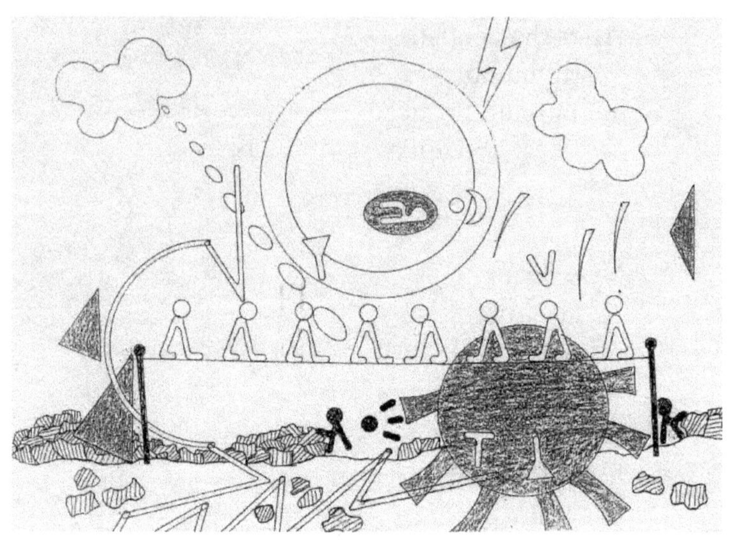

The blank page
before me
begs for words
that I don't have.

* * *

Sometimes meaning increases
        in a million directions
random thoughts and noise
            echo with truth
and unknown definitions

* * *

Eraser…
Smooth one, you,
removing mistakes
        from paper.

If only you could
help to change
        my life.

While editing my story,
I look down
at the words
I've taken out.
There, I find
                    a poem.

* * *

The thread of my story,
tying, untying, retying.
Sleepless nights, dutiful days,
books of other's stories,
years of falling suns and darkened hours.
     Until I'm at the end of string.

* * *

Always imagine
      another sentence.

Teens

They play their music loud,
don't listen to its words,
and dance to drummers
we don't know.

* * *

Simple

It's hard to believe,
so unbelievably simple,
how much you can achieve,
with a whimper and a dimple.

* * *

Student Lounge

At the snack machine,
Eager, hungry, wanting.
Shoving coins and pushing buttons.
Grabbing goodies…Gluttons.

Eileen Kimbrough

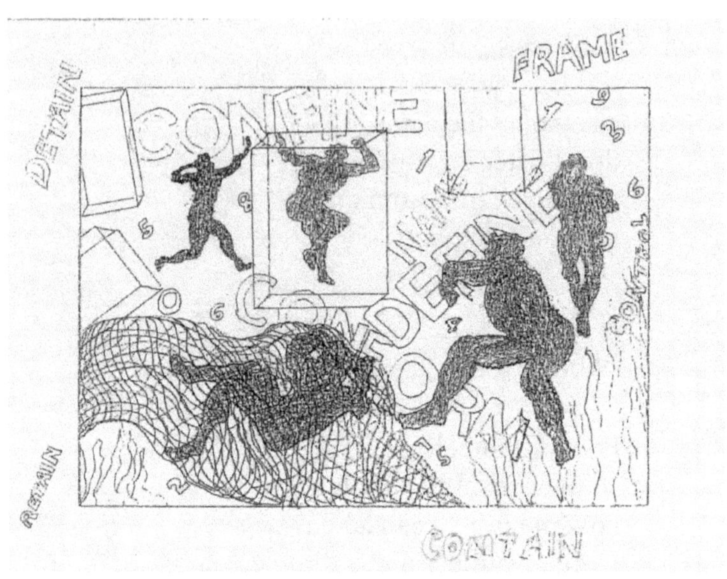

I walk this day
with my shadow.
Later,
  I will lose him.

* * *

They sit on the rooftop,
reading,
just above the eaves.
No one will find them here
or find the place
where they hide
their uncle's magazines.

* * *

The turkey was stuffed
waiting
to burst our bellies.

Eileen Kimbrough

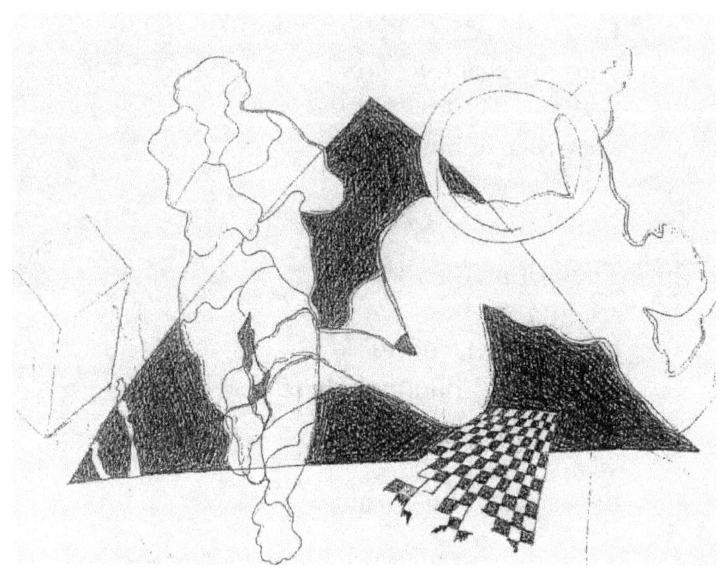

Fear…

I face you every day.
You are always in the way.

* * *

For me, life was always
like an inside joke.
And I was the one
who didn't get it.

* * *

The mirror tells a story
…I don't want to hear.

Eileen Kimbrough

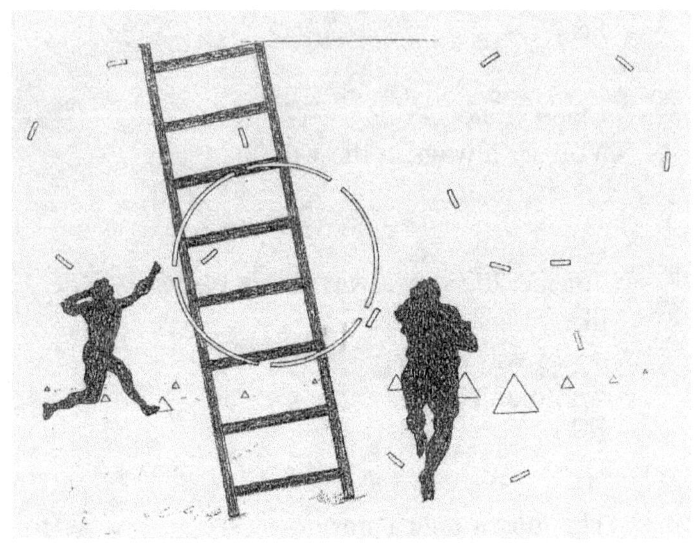

Snoring

Beside me on the bed,
Old snore-monkey
eating up my sleep.

* * *

Dawn

I woke when dawn was breaking.
What I cleaned is now a mess,
My organizing is undone.
My earnings have been spent.
I worked hard and tried
all this broken day.
Then night fell on me.

* * *

Go ahead.
Put me in my place.
I'd like to belong
somewhere.

Imagination

The pickle in a child's hands,
becomes a telephone.
A fork becomes a gun.
Creative minds of youth,
as we watch them
having fun.

* * *

By the living of life,
we are chipped away
splinter by splinter
until what is left
is something new.
Or old, something less,
unless we add to life,
build our strengths
and hone our minds,
learn to live open and large.

The din of music
plays in my ears
long after it stops.

* * *

Echo
In every ordinary moment
thoughts flicker as
we hear the colors of music.
It's a slow deep listening,
until the melody screams,
a cacophony of voices
and honking sax,
the search for a new buzz.
What happens to the echo
when it doesn't answer back?

* * *

Why is…
Abbreviation a long word.
A fly without wings, not a walk.
A doctor's work, his practice.
People who know the least,
know it the loudest.

Eileen Kimbrough

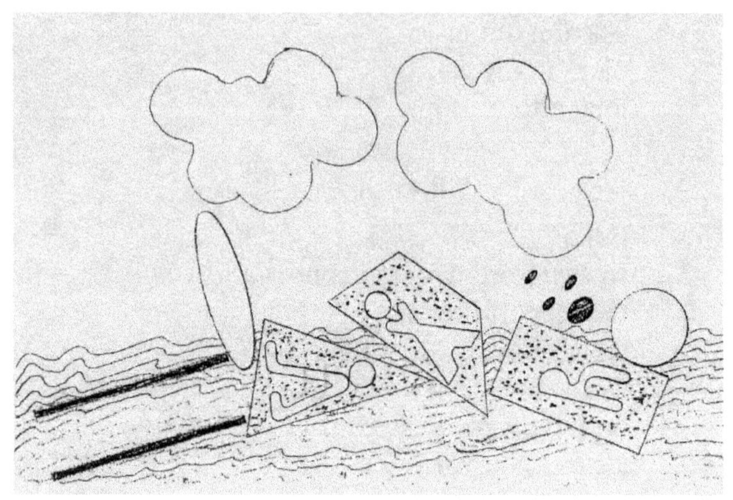

Part Two

Eileen Kimbrough

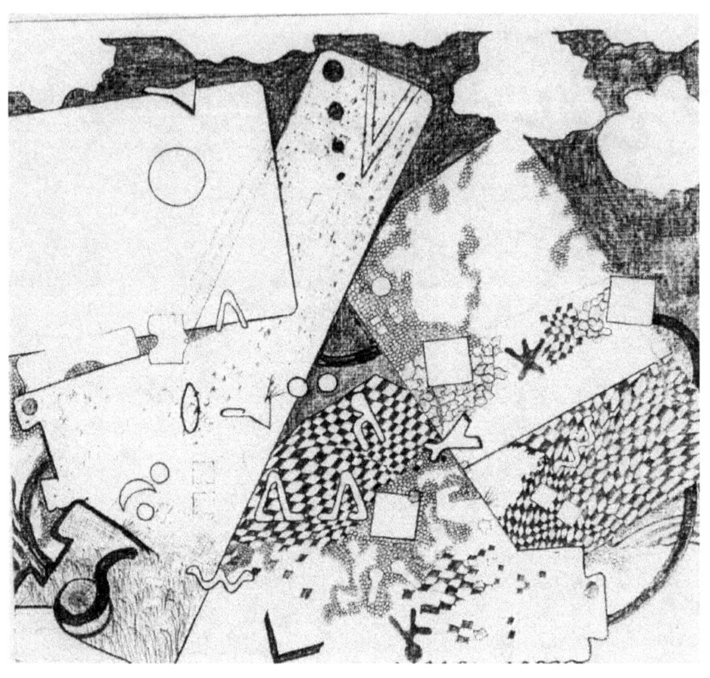

The stars ringing in the sky
are bells of my lost memories
singing their last song

* * *

My heart, a crystal flower,
knows the power of love.
But it's so easy to break.

* * *

Cheated,
the soul
died,
unnourished,
leaving,
a bitter,
empty,
person.

Eileen Kimbrough

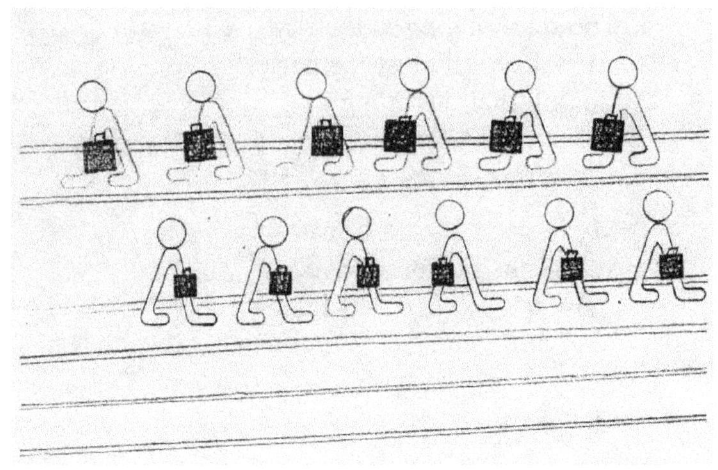

I'm haunted by these ghosts inside,
who hold my fears and pains.
They won't let me forget
the ragged edges of your heart.

* * *

He carved a knife of ice.
The victim screamed and died.
Perfect weapon.
Nothing to hide.
It melted without a trace.
No prints, no clues.
The perfect weapon to use.

* * *

This world is without
unity. When will we learn
that is what it needs?

Apple pieing
chicken frying
self-denying,
traditionalists.

* * *

In the pick-up truck
his cowboy hat, his dog,
and his gun.

* * *

Life gives us lots of lemons
…so many sour people.

On the street
in the rain
cars wiping their eyes.

* * *

Red flashing lights
behind me
I'm caught speeding.

* * *

Under power lines,
trees, chopped, protect energy.
Knobby limbs recall
the old barbaric custom,
amputating hands
that stole bread to stay alive.

Eileen Kimbrough

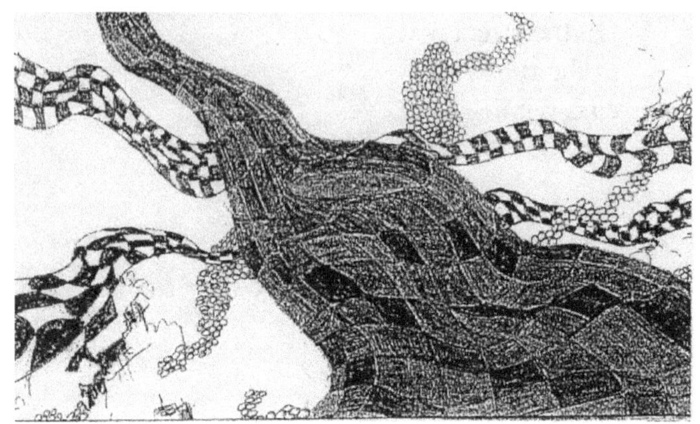

Winter Night

In the starkness of the winter night,
loud sound of a gunshot
down the street.
Death's red fingers paint the snow
where a man fell down without a fight.

* * *

Reasons

Her words bleed envy.
She speaks with a twisted heart.
Her thoughts throw knives
at friends and foe alike.
But she doesn't understand
the reasons she's alone.

* * *

Twilight, end of day
the in-between time
in the nowhere
where shadows lurk.

Eileen Kimbrough

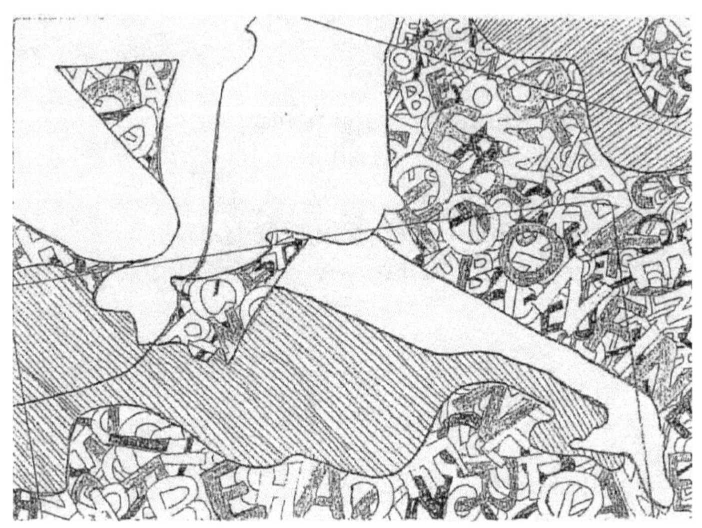

Omen?
The roses in the vase
have lost their petals.
Their stems still stand
this sad day.

* * *

Transformation
Hands, once lovely,
with slender fingers,
smooth skin,
in knots now,
move, twist, stiff.
Perfectionist no more.

* * *

Accommodation:
Women were made for it.

Eileen Kimbrough

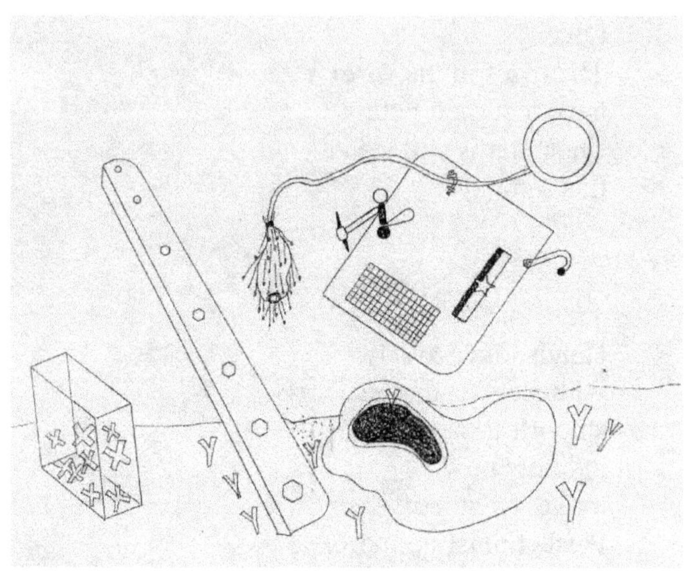

Sometimes life
builds a wall
between my mind
and my pen.

* * *

My poems disappear
as I get out of bed.

* * *

My poems remain somewhere
unfinished, unknown,
until my mind and heart
feel free again.

Teens in speeding cars
think life goes on forever.

* * *

So big, the sorrow that I feel,
the turkey on the table.

* * *

A smile can’t erase
the sadness on one’s face.
Neither can a frown
bring one up from feeling down.

Part Three

Something is never nothing
but nothing can be something.
Nothing is nothing because
we haven't yet discovered
what something it is.

Some things so small
appear to be nothing
but they're not nothing at all.
Many nothings wait to be found,
maybe as something profound.

* * *

I tell the clock, Stand still.
I need more hours, more days.
But the sun and moon keep moving
and I, too, but I don't see it in the hands
or hear it in the ticking clock.
I feel it in the rush of doing what I must
and mostly in things I save for later
but never seem to do.

The sun sends rays from
a silky sky, and I,
enjoy my garden.

* * *

Watch. The firefly flits
over the flower garden
    teasing the kitten.

* * *

Even after sunset,
I can still smell the flowers.

Flowers finally bloomed
only to be swept away
by violent wind.

* * *

Clumps of tulip leaves in my garden
surround the proud stems still standing tall
watching over their wind-strewn petals,
a colorful carpet for the lawn.

* * *

Light…
I can't imagine
life without you.
Like the darkest nights,
unfocused feelings,
touch, without vision.
A different sense of things.
Another way
of knowing.

Under the maple tree
whirling in the wind,
butterflies of life.

* * *

This rainy day
perhaps no one will see
my tears.

* * *

In this tumultuous world
I sit in the stillness
amidst the trees
and contemplate my life.

Eileen Kimbrough

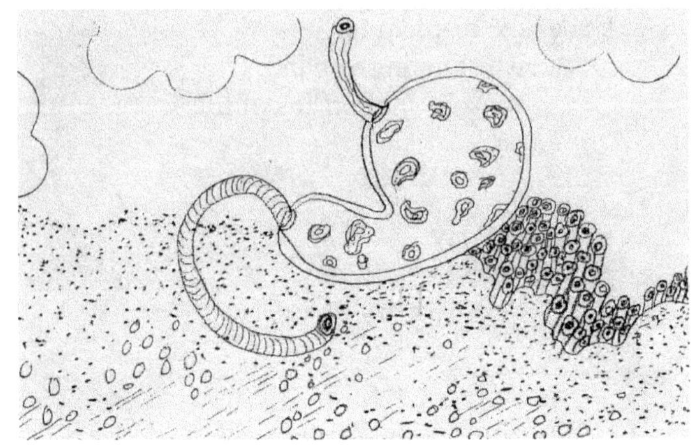

I listen hard but
I can't hear the butterfly.
  See his lovely wings.

* * *

Frogs, groaning, croaking.
chipmunks chirping.
birds, peeping, singing.
leaves rustling in the wind.
water splashing, falling,
music in the garden.

* * *

The heron, waiting
for a jumping fish,
had no lunch today.

Eileen Kimbrough

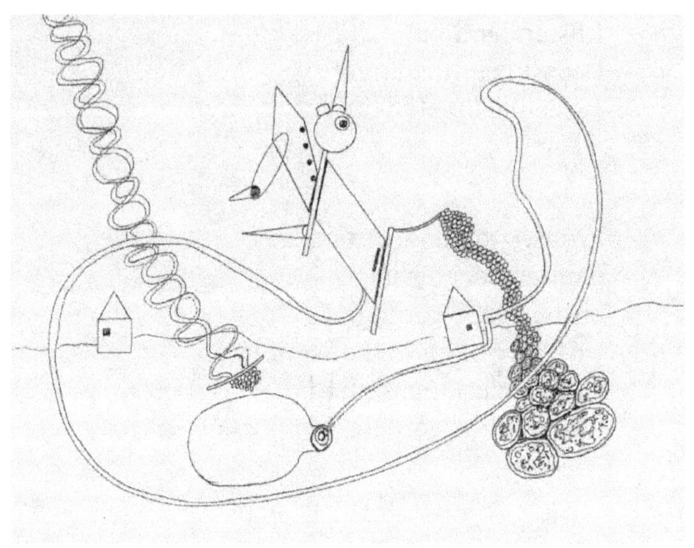

My garden cries, sad,
her flowers have been stoned
with hail.
Stormy spring.

* * *

Look.
Even the broken tree
still bows to the wind
…as if it hadn't had enough.

* * *

The wind-bent weeds grew tall
hiding my flowers.
But the flowers were
protected from the wind.

Wandering through woods
this sunny day.
Listen. Cicada.
            Summer journey.

* * *

Hissing snake in grass.
He moves fast, sees you first.
You must tread lightly.

* * *

The maple in the wind-
    hoping for offspring.

The flowers, so beautiful.
Even so, some people suffer.

* * *

After the rain,
  under the willow tree,
    drops fall.

* * *

Thunder sound
cold spray
wet mist
splashing sounds
flying, singing, water.

Eileen Kimbrough

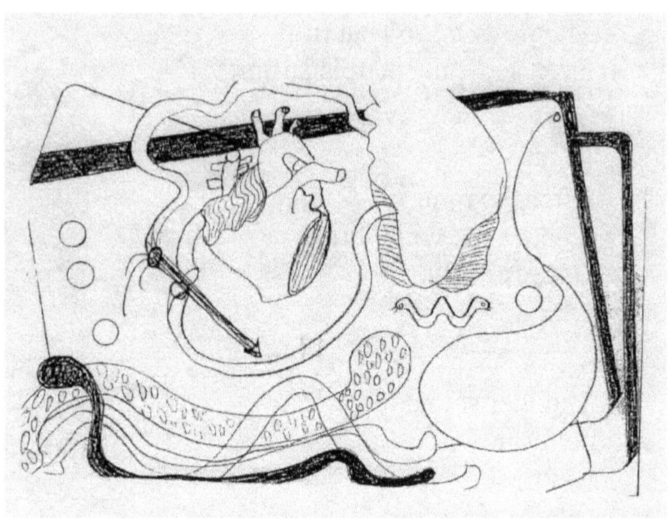

Early spring
in the garden
  a fern unfolds.

* * *

Taking pictures of
flowers and hummingbird.
    That stupid cat!

* * *

See how the flowers
teach the bees to pollinate.
  Or do they trick them?

Eileen Kimbrough

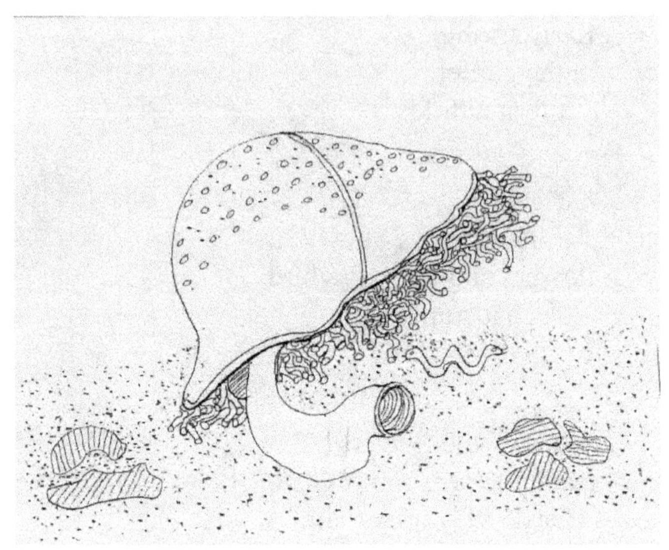

Sunrise. A new dawn.
Don't waste away these fine hours.
Too soon, they'll be gone.

* * *

My little garden pool…
  Mirror for the moon.

* * *

Looking for news
Through piles
of drifting snow.

Eileen Kimbrough

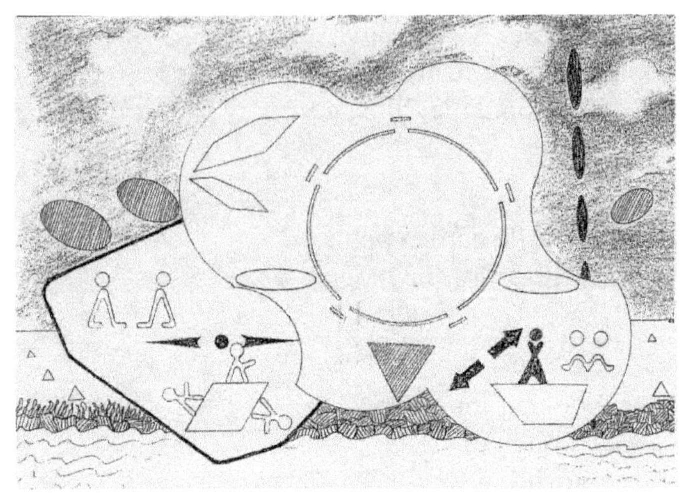

Inside the fruits
of the cherry tree,
tiny beads of life.

* * *

The rain tried so hard,
…but could not make things clean.

* * *

In autumn,
I planted a tulip bulb,
the only sign of hope
that I could find.

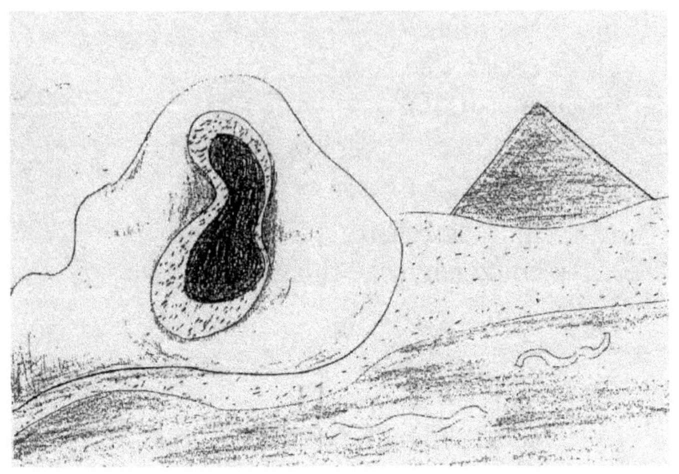

Last snow of spring
weighs down iris leaves.

* * *

The wind swishes the willow
like a wispy paint brush.

* * *

Lady bug crawls across a leaf.
I like her happy dots.

Brr, we say, so cold,
the falling snow in winter.
In summer, we will miss you.

* * *

Branches covered with snow:
Heavily armed trees.

* * *

Fresh snow falling:
Snowman's new clothes.

Gardening,
  is all about time
    and growth
      derived from it.

* * *

Looking into the pool,
  I look back at me.

* * *

Busy hands tend the soil,
pull the weeds,
plant the seeds,
the mind is freed
by busy toil
to dream
and fill the spirit's needs.

Eileen Kimbrough

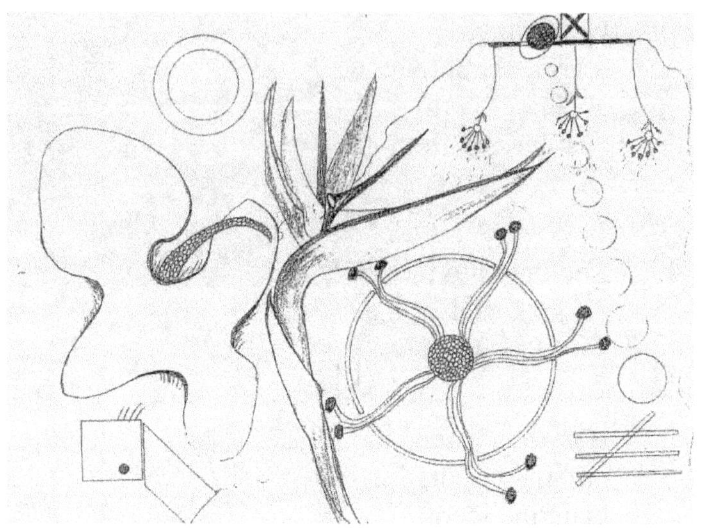

Disappearing starlight
…Dawn arrives.

* * *

Painting the river
  from the west,
    glorious sunset.

* * *

After the rain,
worms on the sidewalk.

Eileen Kimbrough

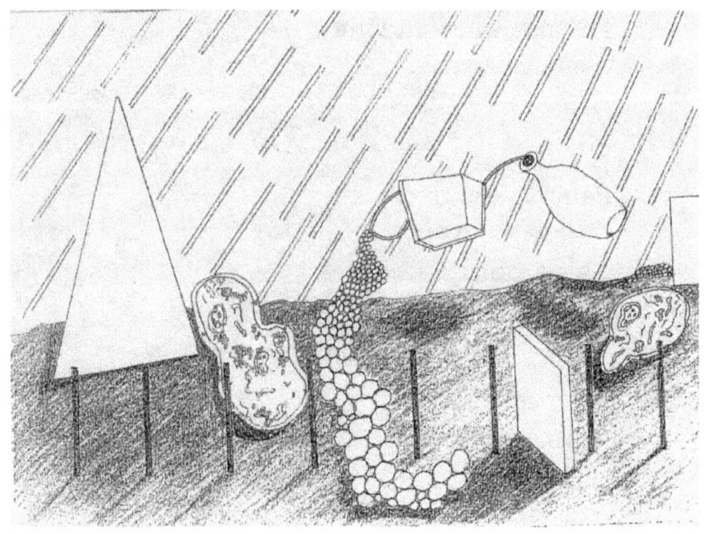

Hanging branch
  of the bridal wreath bush
touches ground,
  sprouts a clone.

* * *

The gray cat
drops a dead bird
on my doorstep.

* * *

Coal eyes, needle beak,
knife wings, cut sky…
          Hawk

Eileen Kimbrough

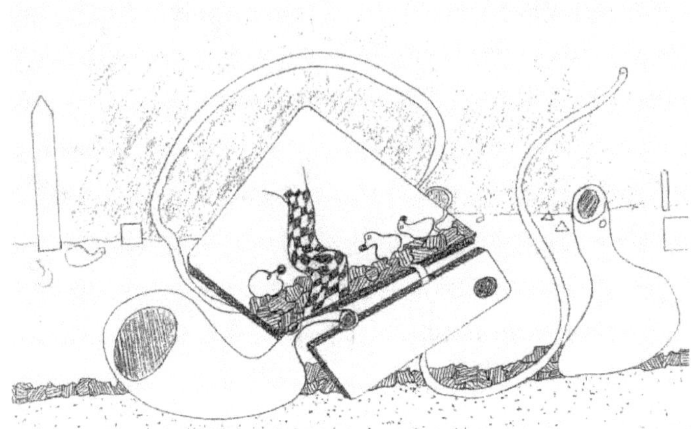

After freeze
  black dandelion
  dead flower
  cold moon

* * *

The flowers on the tree must fall
before the fruit can form.
One beauty displaced by another.
That is the way of the world.

* * *

Even the roses in the vase
can't make me smile today.

Choose your cards carefully.
Hold on to the best.
You're skipping stones for thrones.
Sit high. Don't give in.
You can break the devil's backbone.
Crush his naked lies and untouched truth.
There is only one choice.
The right choice.
It's in your hands.   Hold tight.

* * *

I am a consciousness on a page.
I come alive when you read me.
My words are actors on a stage.
You give them authenticity.

If, as you read, you understand,
and hear the words as I have planned,
then I will live when I am gone,
and so, escape oblivion.

Part Four

Eileen Kimbrough

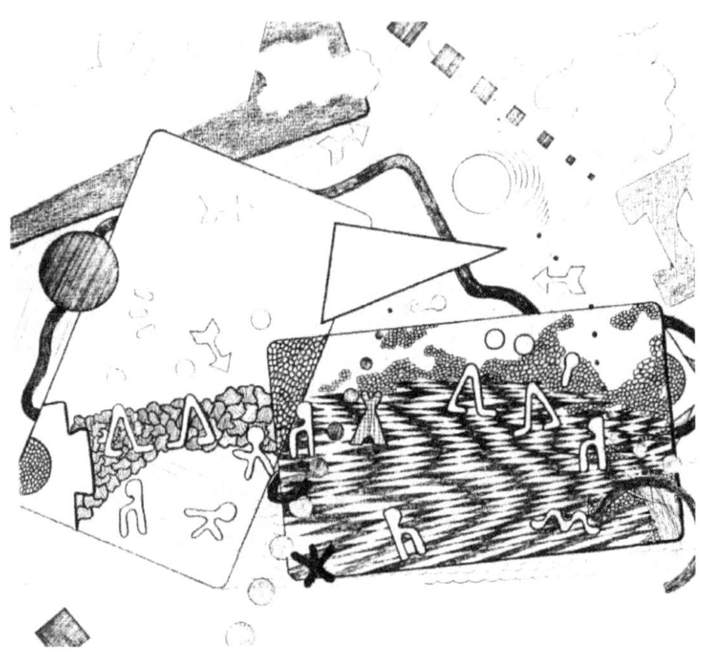

I move cautiously onward
listening to the wind,
looking without seeing.
I've been too long in the dark.
I'm a living metaphor for innocence.

* * *

I am driven by impossible dreams
weaving through smoke and mirrors,
making mistakes along the way.
But I am chasing wisdom.

* * *

Passing

Time is relative
What was then is not now.
But what if then and now
could meet- somehow?
Like passing in the night,
if Moon or Earth slipped a beat,
and my great grandmother and I
might speak.

My life:
A book of moments,
Only ripples in time,
Too soon forgotten.

* * *

I write my life
on pages
small words
great pain

* * *

Hidden Meaning
Shadow beneath language,
    delicate purple whisper,
frantic moment,
        truth over science
                Scream

Writing a Haiku,
  I smile at the words.

* * *

At the roadside,
a flattened squirrel.

* * *

The picture on the cover
  of his book…
I wonder what
  its story is.

Eileen Kimbrough

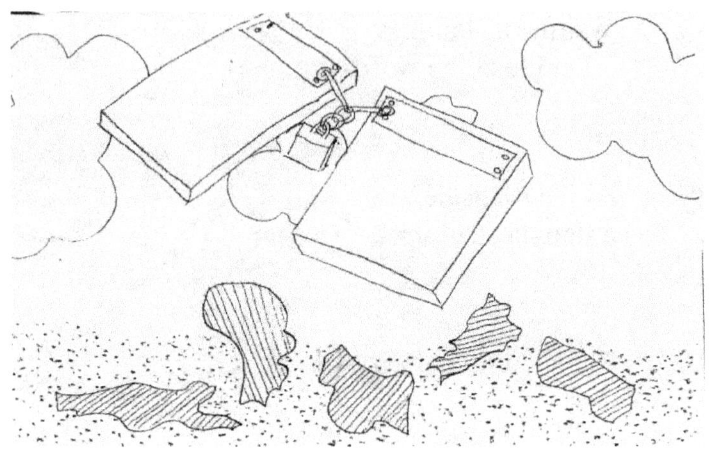

I can't sing.
My father told me that
  when I was five.
When music plays,
  I am silent.
Frozen words
  won't come out.
But I can write a poem
    that he can't read.

* * *

I'm walking over words
that I don't want to hear,
stomping, kicking, crushing them.
They must be wrong! They must!
They tell a truth too sad to bear.

* * *

Let me keep my microcosm of self
with no demon particles.
Let no comfortable liars enter.
Embrace my now. At least it's true!

Eileen Kimbrough

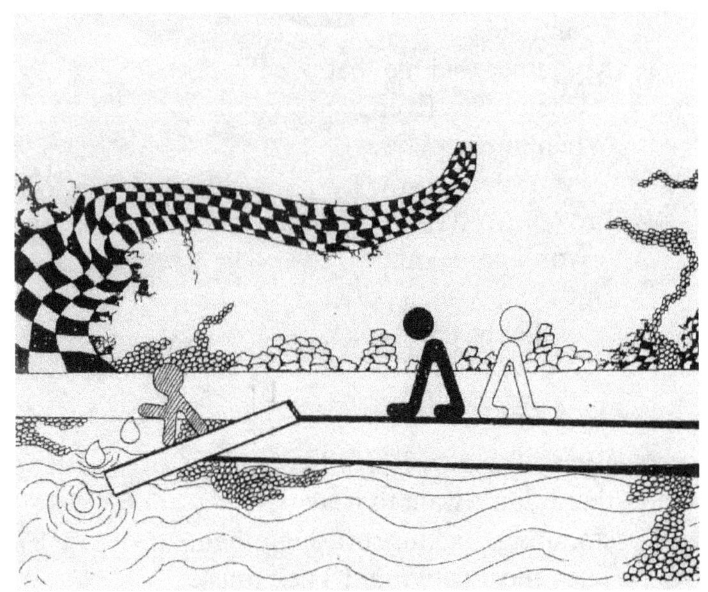

Twilight, end of day
the in-between time
in the nowhere
where shadows lurk.

* * *

All the neon of this night
emits an eerie glow.
Boundaries blur as I
walk in shadows
between reality and dream.

* * *

You never know who you might meet,
perhaps be blown away.
Beware the winds
        about and walking.
There are things you feel
        but do not see.

Eileen Kimbrough

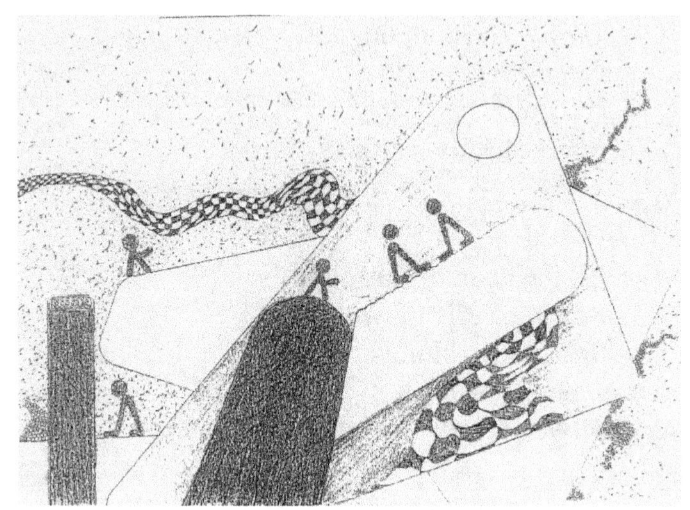

I could never eat
　　　　the chicken
who eats cow-dung
　　and dirty rocks.

Besides, I've seen
　　　　her little eyes
before the hatchet chops

* * *

My heart grows heavy
with broken pride
and I am plunged in darkness,
　　pain's reminder,
as the sky is falling.

* * *

Blankets of loneliness,
the depth of stars,
like a rock in the sun's eye,
the blackness of eternal night.
What is known about dark?

The dark of night
carries us into another world
of sleep and dreams.
A world where forgotten things
mix with fantasies,
where the new and strange
pose as normal.
Where lies disguise themselves
as truth,
  their authors, everywhere.

* * *

I can see that he is fickle.
It's in the eyes
drifting away like that
toward unheard melodies,
unseen, unmet loves,
his uncontrollable desire.

* * *

He left me with
scars beyond skin,
deep within my heart,
mind, and soul. Unseen,
they'll last forever.
  Unlike his love.

Words…
like water, flowed
easily off the tongue,
washing themselves of meaning
as they dropped, falling deep into dirt.
What was thought to be a promise
was only lies told to appease, please.
Instead, causing hurt and broken ties.

* * *

The tears, held back at first,
now rushed and would not stop
The fury of this sorrow's storm
washed away my hope, my plans.
I have no more.

* * *

I need to cut away the masks,
the superstitions,
all empty suppositions.
I've been seduced by false promises.
I want to enjoy the now.

Eileen Kimbrough

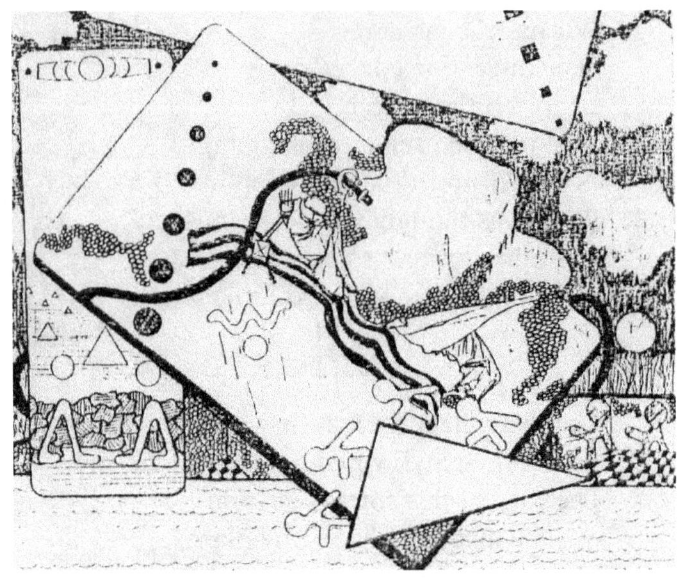

We live in a society of fear,
listening to uneasy voices.
Yet we step over cracks in floors,
climb tall mountains,
ride the rapids of rivers,
and dive over falls.

* * *

Seeds of the future sown,
life so fragile, now
with tainted food and air,
day of birth past,
waiting cradle, empty,
                    but for tears.

* * *

I wake from a dream,
sadly finding everything
     as it was before.

Eileen Kimbrough

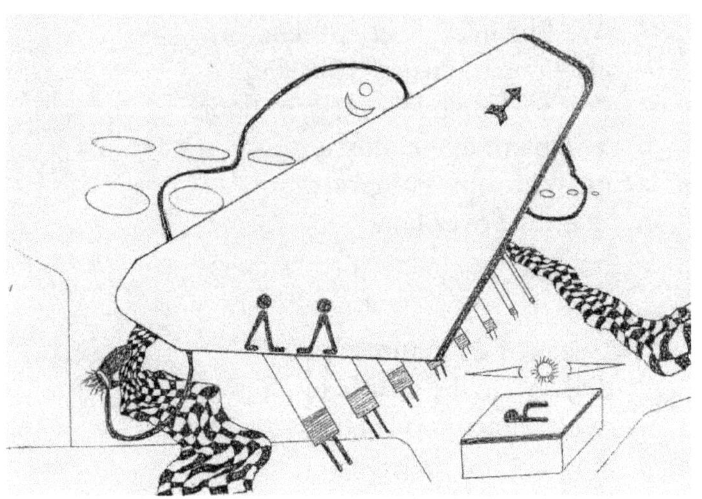

When seeds of reality are sown
our dreams collide,
sending us amongst the grains of stardust
where you are out of reach.

* * *

The sky has lifted
its veil of dark clouds,
opened a new page.
  Aspirations
    can now be
      more than dreams.

* * *

Living on the edge
and testing boundaries,
we sometimes go too far.
There is no yellow light for life.

He walks beside me through the day,
my silent, loyal friend.
When the sun goes down, he leaves,
disappears into the darkness
where shadows go.

* * *

Pretty girls on covers
of hidden magazines.
Dirty minds
turn the pages.

* * *

Do you ever really watch
someone gesture with his hands?
It's like another language
that we read unconsciously.
A language that, when mixed with words,
emphasizes meanings.
We listen with eyes as well as ears.

Sliding through barriers
as if you're the wind,
go ahead. Judge me.
I am a slave to gravity,
not free to roam, as you.
But I am anchored, my soul is free.

* * *

An ocean full of waves,
    the force inside me.
It bursts forth with terror
    and I flee.
The panic of the moment,
    explosion of fear.
leads me away from danger,
    I only feel, but do not see.

* * *

Our knowledge, gone with the wind
in this plastic world
of make-believe and sad clowns
whose titanium tears and sordid so
yesterday's true demons, bring fea
and wash away my hope.
Go ahead, light my candles.
                Burn away my yea

Eileen Kimbrough

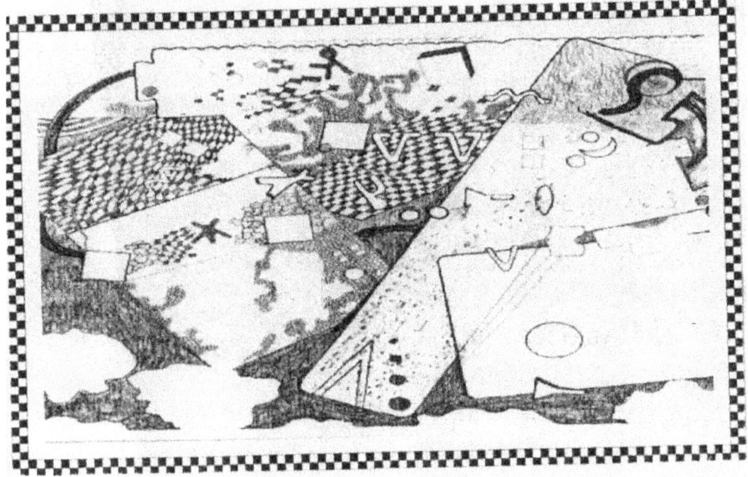

My memories, like my flowers, fade.
They die and disappear.
But like some flowers that rebloom,
some memories return
 …perhaps not quite the same.

* * *

My shadow, not even there,
I hear you laugh.
You're a wind-up toy,
you may hide but can't escape.
 You're attached to me.

* * *

Yellow
I've lived too close to too much
yellow for too long.
Now, yellow is no good for me.
Give me red, purple, pink, instead.
I have been too close
to yellow's toxic head.

Eileen Kimbrough

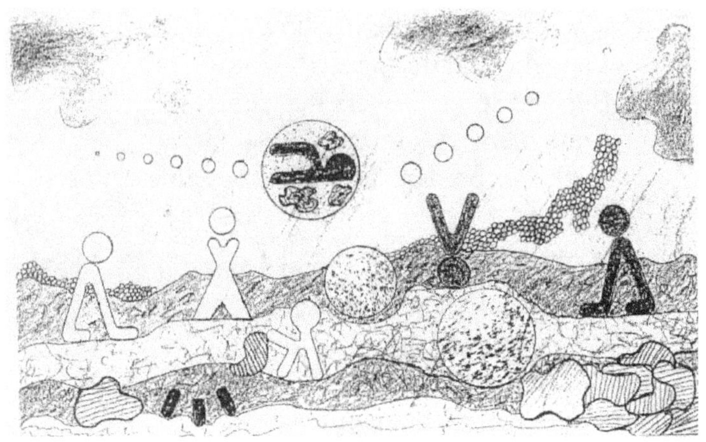

My life

has been one
  red light
after another.

* * *

I know this the best
of many things I know;
Everyone needs love.

* * *

We are all one light
in a room with many windows.

These cruel lights are too intense
showing me the wrong way,
leading me into troubled water
with my back against the wall
as I race against demons you can't see.

* * *

Head in clouds
over the cliffs by needle rock
blackberry clouds bring rain
voice of whirring wind
thunder loud
ticking clock
lots of pain
time to end.

* * *

If I should fail
at what I try
Don't let me crash and die.
Help me fall like gentle rain,
only slightly bruised,
so I can get up and try again.

Combining what I know
with what I wish I knew;
a collage of possibilities.

* * *

We look for truth in lives
untouched by time,
find it only after all our choices
have been made.

* * *

Time, so deep.
We are only one short layer.

* * *

Haikus disrobe one's thoughts,
leaving only what is real.

Eileen Kimbrough

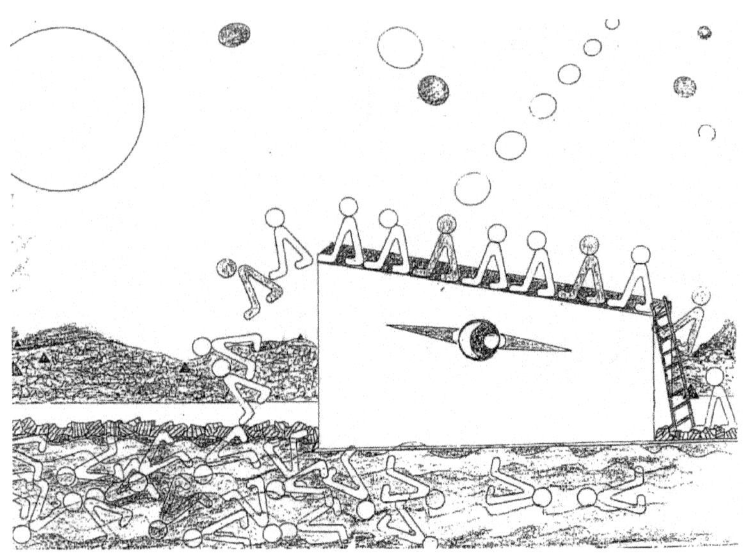

www.ingramcontent.com/pod-product-compliance
Lightning Source LLC
LaVergne TN
LVHW010628100826
845148LV00014B/3159